Happiness

➹➾❮❮

Marcus Aurelius

Happiness

HOW TO ACHIEVE IT

→>-<←

P

PROFILE BOOKS

First published in Great Britain in 2001 by
Profile Books Ltd
58a Hatton Garden
London ECIN 8LX
www.profilebooks.co.uk

Introduction and text selection copyright
© Jeremy Scott 2001

Text extracts selected from the *Meditations* of Marcus Aurelius;
Casaubon translation of 1635.

The moral right of the author has been asserted.

A CIP catalogue record for this book is available from
the British Library.

ISBN 1 86197 367 5

Cover design by the Senate
Cover and frontispiece illustration by Clifford Harper
Text design by Geoff Green
Typeset in Van Dijck by MacGuru
info@macguru.org.uk

Printed and bound in Great Britain by
Bookmarque Ltd, Croydon, Surrey

Contents

Introduction   7

Marcus describes how he came to evolve
   his method   18

Preparation for the method   24

Elect reason to be your ruler   26

Practice of reason and understanding   28

Examination and analysis   34

Attitude   40

Purpose   48

The dogmata   52

On the art of living in the world   54

Dogmata on the use of reason and
   understanding   62

Dogmata on your own flaws   72

Dogmata on purpose and intention   76

Dogmata on the character of politicians   80

Dogmata on your own essential nobility   82

The three possibilities … and after   86

Marcus sums up   92

S ome people are born with a silver spoon in their mouth. When Marcus Aurelius entered the world in AD 121 his infant lips held not just one but three.

His paternal grandfather, a senator, was Prefect of Rome; his maternal grandmother was heiress to a huge family fortune; and, most significantly, his aunt was married to Antoninus Pius, who would become the next emperor. A direct descendant of Numa, the second king of Rome, Marcus's future held considerable promise.

And also unusual risks. The Roman Empire was vast, reaching from the Middle East to Scotland, from Germany to the coastal states of North Africa. It was ruled by a succession of emperors who held absolute power. Many were tyrants, some murderous and mad, others intoxicated by cruelty. Their opportunity for self-indulgence and perversity was unlimited. Caligula tortured and beheaded people from pure caprice and seriously considered the butchery of the entire Senate. Nero illuminated his evening parties with live, burning Christians, and sometimes diverted himself at ·

night by roaming the streets in disguise, slashing the throats of lone pedestrians.

Marcus, whose father had died when he was a baby, was brought up in the house of his grandfather, who for most of his life held public office. He was not sent to school, as was usual for noble youths, but educated at home by several tutors. As a result he was not influenced by the atmosphere of the schools, which reflected the extravagance, competitive ostentation and permissiveness of most noble families at that time.

Marcus's teachers were the best and his education intensive; he proved a diligent student. Since Plato had laid down the ideal study-programme five hundred years earlier, high value had been placed on physical training, strength, balance and co-ordination. Marcus boxed, wrestled and ran. He was an excellent ball-player and enjoyed the excitement of hunting boar, though later he would lose his taste for this.

At the age of eleven he started on the study of Stoic philosophy, which had developed from the thinking of Plato and Zeno. This was a method of achieving wisdom and self-reliance by means of certain mental and physical disciplines. Marcus writes that the Stoic philosophy taught him to 'prefer a plank bed and skin' to greater comforts. (And it's said that the skin was only a concession to his mother, as he would have preferred to sleep on bare boards or on the ground.)

At seventeen Marcus was adopted by Antoninus as his son and trained to become emperor in turn. He was twenty-four when he married his cousin Faustina, the daughter of Antoninus. Eventually, aged forty, he inherited the job of emperor on Antoninus's death. His first public act was one of remarkable generosity. Usually a new emperor would kill or exile any potential rival to power, but instead Marcus gave his adoptive brother, Verus, a share in his rule, making him a tribune and proconsul, and awarding him the title of Caesar.

Marcus had a large family of eleven children by Faustina, and in the first year of his reign she bore twins. One would die, but the survivor later became the wicked and detested

Emperor Commodus. As though the birth were an omen, a storm of disasters at once burst over the long tranquil state of Rome. The Tiber flooded, destroying a great part of the city, the waters drowning cattle, spoiling the harvest, wrecking fields and causing widespread famine. Earthquake and a plague of insects followed. Then the Parthians invaded the Roman province of Syria, defeating a Roman army. Next, the wild tribes of the Catti rampaged through Germany with fire and sword. Meanwhile, from Britain, on the empire's western frontier, came news of insurrection and disorder.

As the Parthian war was the most crucial of the three conflicts, Marcus sent an army under the command of Verus to regain Syria. It was successful, but the victorious troops returning home brought the plague with them. For years afterwards this terrible pestilence raged through the empire, killing thousands, including Verus.

Such was the nature of Roman society that the defamatory rumour spread that Marcus had ordered his brother's death – just as, later, whispers would circulate about Faustina's infidelity. Both rumours were inspired by malice and were ignored by Marcus, but his disillusion with the people surrounding him sometimes breaks out in his *Meditations*: 'A black character, bestial, childish, stupid, effeminate, counterfeit, scurrilous, fraudulent … And the things which are much valued in life are empty, and rotten, and trifling, and little dogs biting one another, and little children quarrelling, laughing and then straightway weeping. But fidelity, and modesty, and justice, and truth are fled from this earth.'

From a population demoralised by the plague Marcus managed with difficulty, and only by enlisting slaves, to raise a new army, which he led north to secure the Danube frontier. While he was doing so, a ragged horde of German tribes invaded Italy itself, seizing a strategic stronghold on the Adriatic coast. Leaving his forces still engaged in heavy fighting in the north, Marcus hurried back to Rome to levy yet another force to recapture the Adriatic territory. The expense of these wars had exhausted the imperial treasury. The state was effectively bankrupt, its government impotent and the morale of the population at a critical low.

Marcus resolved this desperate situation by a brilliant stroke of public relations. In a huge public auction he sold off the ornaments and fittings of his imperial palace. His wife sold much of her jewellery. The funds realised turned around the economy, restored morale, raised a new army and saved the empire. Nevertheless, it was with a heavy heart that Marcus set off on the long march to Germany at the head of his new forces. On the eve of departure his little boy, twin brother to Commodus, had died.

The campaign against the barbarian tribes, fought in difficult, mountainous terrain, was attended by many dangers. Early in the war, as Marcus was testing the depth of a river crossing, he was attacked by a hail of missiles and only saved from death by being sheltered beneath the shields of his soldiers. The most significant event of the war, however, resulted in victory, becoming known as 'the miracle of the thundering legion'.

Marcus and his army had been caught in a steep mountain pass, into which they had been lured by a sham retreat of the enemy's archers. Trapped there, unable either to retreat or fight, tormented by heat and thirst, under a rain of arrows and stones from the surrounding heights, the Roman soldiers lost all hope and gave way to despair.

At the most critical moment a storm burst overhead, accompanied by thunder and lightning. Heavy rain fell, which was caught by the soldiers in their shields and helmets and used to quench their own and their horses' thirst. While they were doing this, the barbarians attacked in force. But the driving rain had now turned to hail, slanting full into the faces of the enemy and blinding them.

The result of the engagement, which ended in the total rout of the barbarians, with no losses on the Roman side, was attributed to divine intervention, and the force was renamed 'the thundering legion', their shields henceforth marked with a zigzag bolt of lightning.

Marcus had no time to enjoy a respite. His army was mopping up the supporting tribes and establishing garrisons to control the area when he received news that his trusted general Cassius, commanding the army in Syria, had rebelled and was supported by his forces. Cassius had proclaimed himself emperor in Marcus's place, and in Rome there were men ready to back him, but he proved unable to retain the allegiance of his soldiers in his new role. After only three months he was assassinated by a group of his own officers.

His head was cut off and sent to Marcus, who received it with no pleasure, for the general had been a close friend. As ever he behaved generously, requesting the Senate to pardon Cassius's family, send no one into exile and take no reprisals. He then travelled to Syria, visited the territories which had supported his rival and pardoned their forces. In this way the ashes of the rebellion were quietly but effectively extinguished. At army headquarters in Syria, Marcus was given the correspondence of Cassius from before and during the conspiracy. In a gesture of remarkable magnanimity he threw the bundle of letters into the fire unread.

It was during this time that Marcus's wife Faustina died. There was a strong rumour that Cassius had acted as he did only because of her encouragement. Marcus ignored this story, as he had the reports on a dancer, a gladiator and other lovers with whom Faustina had had affairs during his many absences at the front.

Marcus was a good man, patient and forgiving. Months and years were spent commanding his armies in the many wars which troubled his reign, but when in Rome he devoted his time to justice and administration. Records of his legislation show his major concerns: selection of the most capable officials to run the far-flung Roman provinces; the appointment of suitable guardians for orphans and minors; the emancipation of individual slaves into free women and men. He was described as 'an emperor most skilled in law', and involved himself in many areas, even attempting to solve Rome's chronic traffic problem – to which no one up to the present day has ever succeeded in finding an answer.

The one stain upon Marcus's rule is the harsh persecution of the Christians in Lyon and

Vienne in central France. In his *Meditations* Marcus mentions the Christians only once, commenting on their indifference to death, which strikes him as not noble but obstinate. Yet it is probable he shared the distrust of them felt by most Romans of the period. Possibly what happened in Lyon and Vienne was not on his direct orders. And the fact that many Christians served in his army and no persecutions took place against them in Rome itself during his reign tends to clear him of the charge.

Soon after these repressions in France, fresh uprisings in Germany recalled Marcus to his northern frontier. He was growing old now, and he was tired and unwell. At the start of the spring campaign he fell seriously ill and sent for his son Commodus, asking him to take charge of the war if he died.

Perhaps he had cancer, perhaps the plague. After six days without eating he summoned his friends and Commodus, saying, 'I must say farewell to you, as I go on ahead.' A little later, when the duty officer asked for the day's password, he said, 'Go to the rising sun, for I am already setting.'

A man who sought peace both for his people and within himself, Marcus nevertheless spent much of his time at war. It was while on these military campaigns that he noted many of the 'Meditations' which compose his method to happiness. They were jotted down in his tent at night by lamplight while he camped with his army in hostile country far from Rome. Obliged by circumstances to be a military commander and by history to be an emperor, he was first and foremost a philosopher.

Marcus led an active, stressful life in demanding times. And his health was not good; suffering from a chronic ulcer, he was frequently in pain. He knew his full share of human suffering, including the death of a child and of a well-loved if faithless wife. He had experience of life's reversals as well as its destabilising bounty of vast wealth and absolute power. In the search for happiness Marcus is a reliable guide, for he writes with the authority of first-hand experience. He's been there.

Marcus describes the influences and people that have made him what he is ... and how he came to evolve his method

✦

From my grandfather I learned to be gentle and to refrain from all anger and passion. Of my mother to intend no evil, to content myself with a spare diet, and to avoid all such excesses as come with great wealth. From Rusticus I learned never by way of ostentation to swish about the house in my long robe, or brag; and quickly to be friendly again with those who offend me.

Of him that brought me up I learned to endure hard work; not to need many things; when I have any thing to do, to do it myself, and not to meddle with many businesses.

Of Diognetus not to busy myself with vain and silly things and not easily to believe those things commonly spoken by know-alls and impostors, and above all to use my reason in each and every matter.

From Apollonius, invariable steadfast-ness, and always, whether in the sharpest pains, or after the loss of a child, or in long diseases, to be always the same man. Of Sextus, to be grave without affectation, tender and conscientious with my friends, and not to be offended by idiots.

From Alexander the grammarian, not to rebuke anyone for a social error or mispronunciation, but deftly to utter it as it should be spoken, or courteously and indirectly to do it some other way. From Fronto, how much envy, fraud, pretension and hypocrisy surround a leader, and how the ruling class are somehow incapable of natural human feelings and affection.

Of Alexander, not to put off those duties we owe to friends and acquaintances by the excuse of urgent work. Of Catulus, not to condemn any friend's criticism though it be unjust; and to love my children with true affection. From my brother Severus, to be thoughtful and loving to all them of my house and family. He it was also who did first make me desire to rule a kingdom in which nothing is more important than the good and welfare of its subjects. Of him also I learned to be generous in the largest measure, always to hope for the best, and to be confident that my friends love me.

From Claudius Maximus, to have control over myself in every matter, to be cheerful and courageous in all sudden chances and accidents, as in sickness; to love mildness and moderation, and to do my work, whatsoever it be, thoroughly and without petulance.

In my father, I observed how free he was from vanity, and how ready to hear any man. Also how he did abstain from all unchaste love of youths; never would he neglect or disdain his friends and grow weary of them, nor at any time be too madly fond of them. In those things which concerned his ease and comfort (plenty whereof his fortune did afford him) he was without pride and bragging; he freely enjoyed them, yet when they were absent he found no want of them.

Moreover my father could not endure to be flattered; never wont to use the baths at inconsiderate hours; no builder or constructor of monuments; never finicky about his food or clothes, nor follower of fashions. And whensoever he did any thing it was in such a way that no man could say he did sweat about it, but without fuss, effectively and agreeably.

From the gods I received good parents and good masters; that I was not long brought up by the concubine of my father; that I preserved the flower of my youth and took not upon me to be a man before my time. And that I never had to do with Benedicta and Theodotus, yea and afterwards when I fell into some fits of love I was soon cured.

From the gods also, that as often as I had a purpose to help and succour any who was poor or fallen into some present need, I was not answered by my officers there was not enough ready money to do it; and that

I myself never had occasion to require like succour.

Moreover that I lived under the rule of my lord and father who would take away from me all pride and vain-glory and showed it not impossible for a Prince to live without a troop of guards and followers, rich elaborate clothes, flaming torches, statues, and other like pretensions of government and magnificence.

Lastly, I am grateful I have a wife so loving and ingenious; and that when I did first apply myself to philosophy, to study wherein happiness does consist and the means to attain unto it, I did not fall into the hands of so-called gurus or spend my time reading the manifold volumes of intellectuals, nor similar fashionable nonsense.

All these things, without the assistance of the gods, could not have been.

Preparation for the method

✦><✦

Whatever I am is either flesh, or life, or REASON. Allow not your mind any more to be distracted or swept to and fro. Think little of your flesh, a pretty piece of knit and twisted work made up of bones and skin, nerves and veins; think no more of it than so. And as for your life, consider what it is exactly: a wind. Not one steady wind either, but at every moment let out and sucked in again. And then there is REASON, your ruling part, and here consider well . . .

*Elect reason to be
your ruler*

-+><+-

Allow not your excellent REASON to be brought into subjection to anyone and to become slavish. Do not allow it to be jerked up and down by emotions and unreasonable responses as if attached to wires. Suffer it not to be dejected at any thing now present, or to fear and fly any thing to come.

Your REASON is no one's slave, it is yours. So let these words that follow suffice you; let them be unto you as your general rules and precepts ... your METHOD.

Practice of reason and understanding

→>←

You must be taught before you can either read or write. And much more so is this true about life. For you are born a mere slave to your senses and brutish affections; you are destitute, until you find the teaching of true knowledge, which will bring you to REASON and sound UNDERSTANDING.

The personal reward these provide

The natural property and privilege of an Individual equipped with REASON and UNDERSTANDING is that they reap and benefit from their own fruit; whereas plants, trees and unthinking people, whatsoever fruits they grow are eaten or discarded by others and of no nourishment or good to themselves.

How they lead to liberty
of mind

That man or woman who honours above all things their REASON and UNDERSTANDING (trusting in their own Spirit and the sacred wisdom which issues from it) shall never lament and exclaim, never sigh, never want either solitude or company. And what is chiefest of all they shall live without unsettling desires and without fear.

It is REASON that brings them to this happy place; this is what it means to be free.

Their fertility ...

REASON and UNDERSTANDING are a vine which grows to yield universal fruit for the use of others, but also a precious and secret fruit for yourself to enjoy alone with much profit and satisfaction.

... *and productive nature*

Your REASON has a generous and outgoing nature; it begets to others and benefits them. In such a way it does grow and multiply in abundance, both within you and in the world about you.

Examination and analysis

—>—<—

Fancy not to yourself things future as though they were now present; but of those that are present take those which you most value aside and consider them particularly. Think how wonderfully you would want them if they were absent.

But take heed that, if you do settle your contentment in things present, you come in time so to overvalue them that the lack of them (whensoever this occur) should be a trouble and vexation unto you.

Collect yourself into yourself, so your Soul may by that means achieve tranquillity and rest fully satisfied and grounded in itself without need of any other thing.

Keep an open mind

Keep an open mind, remain flexible.

Remember that sometimes to change your mind and to follow one that can correct your error is just as astute as to be able to discern the right course without advice.

Nothing is beyond the scope of your own deliberation, judgement and understanding.

Query others' actions . . .
and your own

Look around you at others at work, at home, and in their lives and consider this: *very many of the things they both speak and do are unnecessary.*

Then, having identified these things, eliminate them in yourself and it follows that you shall save yourself much time and trouble and foolish busyness.

Before each of your own actions step back and ask yourself this: is not this thing I am about to do unnecessary?

Apply this question not just to actions but to thoughts and plans. Interrogate yourself on each and every one of them and query your intention. Thus the foolish and unnecessary action which would follow will be cut off and you shall always be a gainer.

Examine every proposition before acting

As every proposition or opportunity presents itself unto you consider what it reduces to, that is to say what it really is. Take it apart and examine it.

What different elements make it up? What is its real purpose in this world? Who does it benefit, whom does it harm? How long will it hold good?

Then, without being led astray by others, speak that which seems unto you most true and just; only speak it kindly, mildly, and without hypocrisy.

But before each of your actions pause and put this question to yourself: After it is done, how will this agree with me? Shall I have no occasion to repent it afterward?

Good and evil deeds

Virtue and wickedness consist not in emotions but as actions. In the same way the true good or evil of a reasonable individual are expressed not by their thoughts and feelings but in specific deeds.

Do nothing without examining it closely before you act.

Attitude

+>-<+

Marcus shows that events are merely events, in themselves neither good nor bad. It is your attitude towards them which defines them so — and defines your own character.

The things that affect us . . . they stand outside us and as it were outdoors, neither knowing anything themselves nor able to utter anything unto others concerning themselves.

What is it therefore that passes verdict on them? The ATTITUDE. And that is yours to order for it is subject to your command.

Anxiety

Remember that every thing which troubles you depends only upon ATTITUDE. Change your ATTITUDE and then, as a ship entering harbour, you shall find calm. All things become safe and steady in a tranquil bay protected from storm and tempest, where you may rest in peace.

The key to freedom

Many of those things, which vex or restrict or imprison you it is in your own power to cut off, for they depend merely on perception and opinion. So do so – then you shall find room enough and freedom.

Possessions, lifestyle, status

Receive possessions, advances, and other temporal blessings without ostentation and bragging when they are sent you, and you shall be able to part with them with readiness, no pain, and gracefully when they are taken from you again.

Never flaunt your good fortune and you will not look a fool if it should leave you.

Misfortunes

'This day I did come out of all my trouble.' Nay, I have cast out all my trouble, it should rather be. For that which troubled you, whatsoever it was, lay within your own ATTITUDE – from whence it must be cast out before you can truly and constantly be at ease.

Frustrations

It will but little avail you to turn your anger and indignation upon the things themselves that have fallen cross unto you. For you shall but make yourself a laughing stock, both unto others and to the gods.

Taking offence

Whenever you are offended by someone's wrongful action ... step back to reflect upon yourself and consider if you are not sometimes guilty of the same thing.

For, if you do this, then you shall soon forget your anger. Especially if you consider that it was only that person's basic stupidity, or else their ignorance, which caused them to do such a thing in the first place.

The impregnable nature of the disciplined mind

They kill me, they cut my flesh, they persecute me with curses . . . So what?

May not your mind, despite all this, continue pure, lucid, balanced, just? As a fountain of clear water, though she be cursed by some stander-by, yet her spring does still run as sweet and clear as before. Yea, even though dirt or dung be thrown in, yet this is at once dispersed and swept away. She cannot be polluted or affected by it.

What then must I do so that I may have within myself an overflowing fountain and not a muddy well?

Beget yourself by continual thought and practice to true liberty with good will to others, and to directness and simplicity without pretension.

A citadel which can never be conquered

Remember your mind is altogether uncon-querable. When once fully collected and grounded in herself, she cannot be over-come by any external force or argument, however compelling.

Therefore let your chief fort and place of defence be a mind free from passions. A stronger place (wherein to make a refuge and so become impregnable) has no one. Therein is the citadel of Reason, the safe base from which your ATTITUDE may sally forth to conquer.

Purpose

✦➤◄✦

Why should any of these events that happen externally so much affect and distract you?

Give yourself time and opportunity to learn some good and useful skill, and cease roving and wandering to and fro. You must also take heed of another kind of wandering, for they are idle in their actions who toil and labour in this life but have no distinct aim or purpose to which to direct all their actions and desires.

Nobility

Resolve not to be slack and negligent, or arrogant and wanton in your actions; nor argumentative and troublesome in your conversation, nor idly to rove and wander in your fancies and ambitions. Nor basely to contract your soul, or make it slave to the group or another's will; nor boisterously to sally out with it as it were, nor ever to be without purpose, work or study to engage in.

Never to speak anything contrary to justice and truth is the only property of a noble Individual. Such a one can never resent another, nor can they be otherwise than steady, cheerful, and content in how they live.

The heroic life

Live as indifferent to the world, and to worldly objects and opinions as one who lives by themselves upon some desert hill. Indeed, *where* you live matters little, for the world is but one place.

But let the inhabitants of the world behold and see you upheaded, tall. Let them look upon a noble Individual who is living proud and true unto themself. If they do not like it, so what? Let them kill you. Better to die, than live as they would have you live.

The Dogmata

+>-<+

An essential part of Marcus's method lies in the dogmata and its frequent use.

To study and follow his method engenders self-reliance and brings about a state of calm and happiness. But living in the world means being surrounded by constant demands, impressions and distractions. These can get to us, fracturing our Stoic calm.

When this occurs, Marcus recommends withdrawing to your dogmata.

The dogmata exists in a private room within yourself, to which you alone possess the key. A warm, comfortable study, its walls are inscribed with truths — the maxims, perceptions, advice and quotations selected by you, which are most true and most relevant to yourself.

People seek for themselves private places to retire to, such as country villages, the seashore, mountains etc. But such places are unnecessary. At any time it is in your power to retire into yourself and be free from all pressures and disturbance. A person cannot anywhere retire better than into their own soul, particularly if beforehand it has been equipped with those things which may afford them perfect ease and tranquillity. Grant then to yourself this retiring frequently, and thereby refresh and renew yourself.

Let these truths you find within form your DOGMATA. As soon as you shall call them to mind they will serve to purge your soul and send you away strengthened and well pleased.

On the art of living in the world

+>-<+

The true art of living in this world is more like a wrestler's than a dancer's skill. That is, to teach a man or woman that whatsoever falls upon them they may be prepared and ready for it, so that nothing may overthrow them or cast them down.

Hold your DOGMATA always in readiness. Use it in the manner of an all-in wrestler who fights with both hands and feet, rather than a gladiator. For if a gladiator loses his sword he is gone, while the other still has his hand free which he may easily turn and use to achieve advantage.

Concerning focus

Let not your mind wander and heap together in her thoughts the many troubles and grievous calamities which you are subject to as any other. This serves for nothing.

But as any contrary event shall happen, put this question unto yourself: *What is it in this present matter which seems unto me so intolerable?* For you will be ashamed to confess it.

And then call to mind another consideration: Nothing that is past, and nothing which lies in the future can injure you; for the one is gone, the other unknown. Only that which is present here and now can harm you.

On acceptance with dignity

As a pig that squeals and thrashes about when its throat is cut . . . so is anyone who grieves about any worldly thing and carries on in such an absurd fashion.

Equally ridiculous is that person who lies in bed moaning about their problems and the miseries of this mortal life.

Submit to providence willingly and freely, for to submit is a necessity imposed by Nature on all creatures equally. You have no choice, so do so with dignity.

Regarding setbacks

As any event should happen to you by way of cross or calamity, call to mind and set before your eyes the example of other persons to whom this self-same thing did once happen likewise.

Well, what did they do, how did they behave? They sulked, they complained, they blamed.

Will you be like them and snivel in the self-same fashion? Let it be your only care and study to make a right use of all such accidents. For there is good use to be made of them, and they will prove fit matter for you to work upon.

Look within! Within yourself is the fountain of all good. Such a fountain where the springing waters of your understanding can never fail, as you dig still deeper and deeper.

On using reversals

That ruling Spirit which lives within you is so versatile and ingenious that it can easily adapt to events as they occur. Even when these do not go as planned, it differently and profitably employs them.

Whatsoever it is that falls out contrary to your first intentions, even that particular adversity it puts to its own use in such a way as a great fire burns and consumes whatsoever comes in its path. Yea, indeed it is by those very obstructions it is made greater and greater.

On illness

'When I was sick,' Epicurus says of himself, 'I never spoke of it to those who came to visit me. My thoughts were only on how my mind (though naturally affected by my indisposition) might keep herself free from distress and still in possession of her rightful happiness.

'Neither did I wholly trust my body to doctors to do entirely as they wished, nor did I expect much of them or their advice; for my present state, I thought, liked me very well and gave me good content, and peace of mind.'

When therefore in sickness (if you chance to sicken) or in any other extremity whatsoever, endeavour to attain a similar state of mind. Resolve not to depart from your DOGMATA whatever may befall you, and do not give ear to the discourses of silly people and mere doctors.

How the disciplined mind is invulnerable

In the mind of one who is truly self-disciplined and purged you cannot find anything which is foul or impure or, as it were, festering. Nothing that is servile, nothing half-hearted, or pretentious, or malicious. Nothing obnoxious or furtive, nothing concealed.

Such a person no one, not even death, can surprise, destabilise, or overturn.

Dogmata on the use of reason and understanding

❧❦❧

A good eye must be good to see whatever there is to be seen, and not pleasant things only. And a good stomach must digest all kinds of food indifferently, in the same way as a millstone grinds whatever is fed to it; this is the purpose it was made for.

Likewise, sound reason and understanding must be ready to deal with and make use of whatsoever shall happen to you.

How to determine character . . .

At your first encounter with anyone, say to yourself: This person, what things do they consider to be good, and what things evil? What things give them pleasure, and which things unhappiness? What do they consider honest, and what dishonest, and where are their limits? What are their attitudes to life . . . and to death?

Thus and thus ask yourself. For, knowing these, you will know the way that person will act in every situation.

. . . and motivation

As often as you see any man or woman do anything, say unto yourself: What is this person's underlying purpose in this action?

But begin this course with yourself first of all and diligently examine yourself concerning whatsoever you do.

On the examination of others

Analyse in detail those that you must deal with. Isolate and examine all their actions. Study them in the act of eating, discover how well or badly they sleep. Consider them shitting, and in the act of lust; complacent in the midst of their pomp and glory; and how they behave when angry, rebuking others from the height of some imagined superiority . . .

How base, slavish and contemptible they are! And how little all they do will count for very soon when death has seized them.

On desiring the admiration of others

You must continually ponder and consider with yourself what sort of persons they be whose good word and testimony you desire.

For then will you find no longing for their applause, once you do but penetrate into the true nature of their attitudes and desires and know them naked for what they are. Nor will you so slavishly respect them.

On seeing people as they really are

Those who praise you and applaud your speech, 'O how wisely spoken!' and talk extravagantly well of you, they are but leaves. And those others who curse you and those that secretly deride you . . . they too are but leaves rattling in the wind. Their spring comes and they thrive and swell . . . then the tempest blows and they go down.

Why should you try to court and please others, or so earnestly seek after things, or fly from them, as though any were of true importance or should endure forever?

On fear of others' judgement

Sift the minds and understandings of those whose judgement on yourself you stand in fear of. Discover what they judge of themselves. Then judge them yourself, investigating whether their opinion be accurate and of any value, before you pay any heed to what they think or give it any credence.

Regarding fools

What do you think of that person who believes it a matter of great importance to have the approval and applause of stupid people?

And you, why should you wish to please someone you know to be an idiot?

On tolerance and acceptance

All men are made one for another; therefore either teach them better or bear with them patiently.

But if you do teach them, do so gently, with diplomacy and love.

Dogmata on your own flaws

-»><«-

How much time and leisure does he or she gain who is not curious to know what their neighbour has said or done, or has attempted to do.

Only your own actions are worth consideration; that they should be just and true to yourself and your DOGMATA.

Concerning gossip

Spend not your day in idle thoughts and fancies about other people or gossip about their doings, especially in whatsoever is merely curious, or envious, or suspicious, or malicious.

Occupy your mind only with such things which, should anyone ask what you are thinking, you may answer boldly and sincerely, without blushing to confess the truth of it because it is so trivial or ignoble.

On envy

He has a stronger body and is a better wrestler than I. *What then?*

Is she more beautiful, more successful than myself? *So?*

Ask yourself: Do they bear life's setbacks with greater composure? Or put up with other's offences with more patience, understanding and good humour than I do?

So in these things that truly matter, where are they superior to myself?

Dogmata on purpose
and intention

→>-<←

In the morning when you rise from your bed unwillingly, let this thought be present: 'I am getting up to do the things for which I exist and for which I was brought into this world. Or have I been made for this, to lie in the bedclothes and keep myself warm?'

Do you not see the little plants, the ants, the spiders, the bees, working together to put in order their several parts of the universe? And are you unwilling to do the work of a human being, and shall you not make haste to do that which is according to your nature?

On doing good to others

Some individuals do benefits to others only because they expect a return. Some, even though they do not demand a return, are not forgetful they have rendered a benefit; but others count for nothing what they have done but are like a vine which has produced grapes and seeks for nothing more after it has yielded its proper fruit.

In the same way we should do good to others as naturally as a horse runs or a bee makes honey, or a vine bears grapes without considering the fruit that it has borne.

What more do you want when you have done a service to another? Are you not content to have performed an act conforming to your human nature, and must you seek to be paid for it, just as if the eye demanded a reward for seeing or the feet for walking?

Concerning integrity

Never esteem any thing as profitable which shall constrain you to break your word or be untrue to yourself. Nor to hate anyone, to suspect or curse them, or to lust after anything that needs to be concealed from others by walls or veils or deception.

On anxiety about the future

Why should the thought of the future trouble you? For what does it serve to be mistrustful?

Care for nothing but what should be done *now*. And if you can well see your course let no one divert you from it. But if you do not well perceive that course, suspend your action and take advice from the best so you may discern it.

Dogmata on the character of politicians

→>←←

Consider these, your self-professed politicians, the only qualified leaders of the world (as they think of themselves). So full of affected gravity! Such professed lovers of virtue and honesty. O man, what hypocrisy! What rogues they are in their deeds, how vile and contemptible in themselves.

Do any of them forsake their personal ambition that I should admire them? For without a change within, alas, what is all that posturing and ostentation but the delinquency of slavish minds that would make a show and crave applause while they advance themselves.

But if they boast and swagger I, thank God, am not bound to imitate them. The effect of true philosophy is unaffected simplicity and understanding. O keep me free from pretension, ostentation, and vainglory! Let me never behave like a politician.

Dogmata on your own essential nobility and what follows from it, the heroic life

→>-<-

It is high time for you to understand that there is something in you which is nobler and more divine than either your passions, or your sensual appetites and affections, or your worldly ambitions.

What at this moment occupies your mind? Is it fear, or suspicion, or lust, or greed, or any such base ambition?

To do nothing rashly without some distinct end; let that be your first care.

The next, to have no other end than the common good. To do what is good for others enriches and ennobles *you*.

On the governing rule . . .

If it be not fitting, do it not. If it be not true, speak it not. Ever maintain your own purpose, free from the influence of others and from all compulsion and necessity.

This is what it is to live heroically.

. . . *of the heroic life*

Do nothing against your own will or to the harm of others, nor without first examining it thoroughly. And, when you do act, never do so with reluctance or half-heartedly.

Moreover, let your own honour and integrity always rule over you, for nothing is preferable to that true Spirit which lives within you.

Be as one who needs no oath to affirm their words or actions, nor requires anyone to be a witness to them.

The three possibilities . . .
and after

Either Fate, or Chaos, or God. If Fate, it is unavoidable, so why resist?

If Chaos, and all is a flood of mere casual confusion devoid of all order, you have reason to congratulate yourself that in the midst of all this chaos you have gained understanding and reason with which to govern your own life and actions.

If God, then make yourself worthy of the divine help and assistance.

Concerning the existence of God

To them that ask you, Where have you seen God? or How do you know there be a God? I answer first of all that even to the very eye God is in some manner visible and apparent; for instance in Nature.

Secondly, that neither have I seen my own soul and yet I respect and honour it.

Valuing your own nobility

Honour your own soul. Do nothing to trouble that noble Spirit which lives within the temple of your own breast with a multitude of foolish fancies and desires. Obey that Spirit as a god!

Acceptance

Give what you will, and take away what you will, says one that is well taught and truly modest to Him that gives and takes away.

And it is not with grim stout-hearted resolution that they say it, but out of love, acceptance, and humble submission. For with this comes true freedom and great liberty of mind.

Conformity with God

One whose mind runs along with the divine order in conformity with God's will, because of the matching of their own mind and intention with God's providence, may truly be called 'inspired' or the Divinely Noble ... for they are led and driven along as it were by God himself.

Concerning long life . . .

What do you desire? To live long?

Why? To experience your own decline, lose your wits and become senile? Would you then be able to talk, to think and reason with yourself?

Ask yourself: Is this truly a worthy objective to desire?

. . . and death

In each of the various things which habitu-
ally you do in the course of every day,
pause and ask yourself this: What! Because
I shall not be able to do this particular
thing when I am dead, is that really so
great a loss?

Why then should death seem so grievous
to you?

Marcus sums up

❥❥❤❤

This happiness you are seeking can now be yours, and yours from this moment on, except for one thing that prevents it. Your mistrust that it is possible.

But happiness will truly be yours to enjoy and use if you forget all that is past, and for the future apply all your thoughts and intentions to holiness and goodness.

To holiness, by accepting willingly whatsoever is sent you by divine providence. To goodness, by speaking the truth and doing all things justly. Let nothing deflect you, not even your own pampered body and its inclinations.

Be ready and willing to leave all things when the time of your departure comes. Respect only your mind and your divine part, the Soul. Let your only fear be not of ceasing to live but of never beginning to live properly – that is, according to the laws of nature and by your Dogmata, and to God.

Then shall you be worthy of that World from which and for which you were created

. . . and have become a noble Individual indeed.

Consider this. You do consist of three things only: your body, your life, your mind. The first two you have to some extent to take care of, but only the last is subject wholly to your control.

So, discipline your mind so that she may live free and to herself. In such a way you shall pass the rest of your days without troubles or distractions, nobly and generously disposed, and in good favour and conformity with that divine Spirit which is within you.

Live only, I say, as ruler of yourself. All else is outside your control and does not concern you; it is mere smoke.

Conform to Nature – accept. Accept its seasons and whatsoever comes. Have contempt for death. Can death be terrible to one whose actions, be they many or few, are all good? Accept. Death is but a part of Nature, seasonable and natural.

O Reader, as a citizen you have lived and conversed in this great city which is the World. Whether for long or short, what is it to you? You have lived, you may be sure, as long as the laws and orders of the city required.

Why should it grieve you if that same Nature which brought you into the world should now send you out of it? As if the director should fairly dismiss you from the stage, whom he had taken on to act a while.

'O but the play is not yet at an end,' you protest, 'There are but three acts yet completed!'

Yea, you have well said — for in the matter of life, three acts is the whole play.

To set a certain time to each one's acting belongs to Him only who, as he first caused your composition, so now is the cause of your dissolution. Go your way then well pleased and contented . . . for so is He that dismisseth you.

ADIEU.

Other titles from the 'Illuminations' series

Power
by Machiavelli
The notorious master of the subject sets
out his timeless rules on how to get it, use it
and hold on to it.
ISBN 1 86197 353 5

Love
by Vatsyayana
The Indian sage and compiler of the world-
renowned *Kama Sutra* presents his
stimulating and enduring guide to erotic
technique.
ISBN 1 86197 358 6

Faith
by St Paul
The renowned spiritual teacher explains
how to find and keep to the path that leads
to life after death.
ISBN 1 86197 372 1